21st Century Junior Library

WORKING AT A COMPUTER STORE

by Katie Marsico

CHERRY LAKE PUBLISHING * ANN ARBOR, MICHIGAN

CHERRY LAKE
Publishing

Published in the United States of America by Cherry Lake Publishing
Ann Arbor, Michigan
www.cherrylakepublishing.com

Content Adviser: Christopher Ciabarra, President, Network Intercept
Reading Adviser: Cecilia Minden-Cupp, PhD, Literacy Consultant

Photo Credits: Cover and pages 4 and 6, ©Shiningcolors/Dreamstime.com; page 8, ©Mark Harmel/
Alamy; page 10, ©Rmarmion/Dreamstime.com; page 12, ©avatra images/Alamy; page 14,
©Kim Karpeles/Alamy; cover and page 16, ©iStockphoto.com/Andrew_Howe; cover and page 18,
©Victoria Alexandrova, used under license from Shutterstock, Inc.; page 20, ©AVAVA, used under
license from Shutterstock, Inc.

LIBRARY OF CONGRESS CATALOGING-IN-PUBLICATION DATA
Marsico, Katie, 1980–
  Working at a computer store / by Katie Marsico.
    p. cm.—(21st century junior library)
  Includes index.
  ISBN-13: 978-1-60279-513-6
  ISBN-10: 1-60279-513-4
  1. Computer stores—Juvenile literature. 2. Technology—Vocational
guidance—Juvenile literature. I. Title. II. Series.
  HD9696.2.A2M37 2009
  381'.45004023—dc22   2008048309

Cherry Lake Publishing would like to acknowledge the work of
The Partnership for 21st Century Skills.
Please visit www.21stcenturyskills.org for more information.

CONTENTS

Shoppers can choose from many different computers at a computer store.

What Is a Computer Store?

You stare at the shelves all around you. There are computers everywhere! Some computers have flat screens. Others you can carry with you. There are many computer games. Where are you? You are at the computer store!

Computer store workers can help you find what you are looking for.

Some people go to the computer store to buy a computer. Some go to get parts for their computers. Others stop by to have their computers fixed. Workers at the computer store can help you with all of your computer needs.

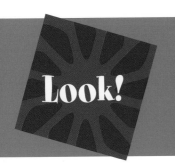

Look!

Look around the computer store. You will probably see items besides computers. What other items are sold there? Hint: Phones and TVs might be two examples.

Computer store workers are happy to spend time answering your questions about computers.

Workers at the computer store have lots of different jobs. **Managers** and **technicians** are two examples. Each worker wants you to have a computer that is easy and fun to use. Are you ready to learn about other workers at the computer store?

Some managers meet with people who are looking for jobs. They decide if a person would make a good computer store worker.

Computer Store Workers

Managers are in charge of the workers. Most stores have more than one manager. Some managers take care of the workers who sell computers. Other managers are in charge of workers who fix computers. Another manager hires the people who work at the store.

Are you trying to decide which computer would work best for you? Just talk to a salesperson!

Will you ever speak to a manager at a computer store? You might! Managers always like to hear what **customers** think of their store.

Who else has a job at the computer store? **Salespeople** can answer some of your questions. They can tell you about what is sold in the store. They can also help you decide which computer is right for you.

Choosing a computer or printer can be hard. That is why workers are there to help!

Computer stores also sell parts such as **printers** or games. These are sold in different sections of the store. Salespeople know the most about the products in their section.

Technicians know how to fix many kinds of computer problems.

Who can you talk to if your computer is not working? You can speak to the store technician. Most computer stores have technicians. They can help fix your computer if it is broken.

Make a Guess!

Guess how many different parts make up your computer. Remember that the technician needs to know how to fix all of these parts. Look for the technician when you are at the store. Ask if your guess was correct.

Some workers help customers when it is time to pay for a computer.

You might also talk to a **customer service** worker. Maybe you bought the wrong item. You want to return it. The customer service worker will help you get your money back.

Do you see why a computer store needs many workers? Everyone there wants to help you find a computer that is right for you!

Do you like computers? Maybe you should think about working at a computer store!

Do You Want to Work at the Computer Store?

A computer store can be an exciting place to work. Learn as much as you can now. This will help you decide if one of these jobs is right for you!

Ask Questions!

Do you want a job at the computer store someday? You can start thinking about this now. Talk to workers when you visit the computer store. Ask them what they like best about their jobs.

GLOSSARY

customer service (KUHSS-tuh-mur SUR-viss) workers at the computer store who can help you if you need to return an item

customers (KUHSS-tuh-murz) people who buy items or pay to have their computers fixed at the computer store

managers (MAN-uh-jurz) men and women who are in charge of other workers at the computer store or in charge of the entire store itself

printers (PRINT-urz) machines that can print information from the computer

salespeople (SAYLZ-pee-puhl) workers at the computer store who help customers decide which computer is right for them

technicians (tek-NISH-uhnz) workers at the computer store who fix computers that are broken

FIND OUT MORE

BOOKS

Cunningham, Kevin. *Computers.* Ann Arbor, MI: Cherry Lake Publishing, 2009.

Somervill, Barbara A. *The History of the Computer.* Chanhassen, MN: The Child's World, 2006.

WEB SITES

U.S. Department of Labor—Bureau of Labor Statistics: Computer Support Specialist
www.bls.gov/k12/computers02. htm
Learn more about what computer technicians do and how they help people

U.S. Department of Labor and U.S. Department of Education—Career Voyages: Information Technology
www.careervoyages.gov/ infotech-main.cfm
Read about different people who work with computers, including salespeople and technicians

INDEX

ABOUT THE AUTHOR

Katie Marsico is the author of more than 50 children's books and lives in Elmhurst, Illinois, with her husband and children. She would especially like to thank Ed Lukens at Micro Center for helping her research this title.